UNLOCKING HAPPINESS

Strategies for Finding Joy in Everyday Life

Harry Jefferson

TABLE OF CONTENT

INTRODUCTION

In a world that often seems consumed by chaos and uncertainty, the pursuit of happiness stands as a beacon of hope—a guiding light that illuminates our path toward fulfillment and well-being. Happiness isn't just a fleeting emotion or a distant goal; it's an essential aspect of our human experience that shapes the quality of our lives in profound ways.

In "Unlocking Happiness: Strategies for Finding Joy in Everyday Life," we will embark on a transformative journey—a journey that transcends mere existence and invites us to embrace the abundance of joy that surrounds us. Through the exploration of proven strategies and practical insights, this book is dedicated to empowering you to unlock the door to happiness and step into a life filled with purpose, passion, and possibility.

As we embark on this journey together, it's important to recognize the significance of happiness in our lives. Beyond its intrinsic value as a source of pleasure and contentment, happiness serves as the cornerstone of our well-being, impacting our physical health, mental resilience, and overall satisfaction with life. From enhancing our immune function to fostering deeper connections with others, the benefits of happiness ripple across every aspect of our existence, enriching our experiences and amplifying our sense of fulfillment.

Yet, despite its undeniable importance, the pursuit of happiness can often feel elusive, leaving many of us feeling adrift in a sea of discontentment and longing. This is where "Unlocking Happiness" steps in, offering a roadmap to navigate the complexities of human emotions and uncover the secrets to lasting joy.

Throughout this book, we'll delve into the very essence of happiness, exploring its complex nature and uncovering the key ingredients that contribute to its cultivation. From understanding the science behind happiness to cultivating a mindset of gratitude and resilience, each chapter is designed to equip you with the tools and techniques needed to harness the power of happiness and integrate it into your daily life.

But our journey doesn't end there. In addition to offering practical strategies for finding joy, "Unlocking Happiness" also invites you to embark on a deeper exploration of self-discovery and personal growth. From nurturing positive relationships to uncovering your unique sense of purpose, each chapter serves as a stepping stone toward a life of greater meaning and fulfillment.

As we embark on this journey together, let us remember that happiness is not a destination to be reached but a path to be traveled—one that unfolds with each moment of awareness and intention. Through the pages of this book, may you discover the courage to embrace your inherent capacity for joy and unlock the boundless potential that resides within you.

So, are you ready to embark on this journey? If so, let's begin. Your path to happiness awaits.

CHAPTER ONE

UNDERSTANDING HAPPINESS

Defining happiness: What is it?

Happiness is such a simple word, yet its meaning is as vast and varied as the human experience itself. At its core, happiness can be described as a state of emotional well-being characterized by feelings of joy, contentment, and satisfaction with life. It is the warm glow that fills our hearts when we experience moments of connection, purpose, and fulfillment.

However, defining happiness is not a straightforward task, for it is a concept that transcends mere words and defies rigid categorization. While some may equate happiness with fleeting moments of pleasure or material wealth, true happiness is more profound—it is an enduring sense of inner peace and alignment with one's values and aspirations.

To truly understand happiness, we must look beyond surface-level definitions and delve into its essence—the intangible essence that resides within each of us, waiting to be discovered and nurtured. It is a journey of self-discovery—an exploration of the heart and soul—that leads us to the realization that happiness is not something to be pursued externally but rather a state of being that emerges from within.

Exploring the science of happiness

In recent years, scientists and researchers have turned their attention to the study of happiness, seeking to unravel its mysteries and uncover the factors that contribute to its attainment. What they have discovered is both illuminating and empowering, shedding light on the inner workings of the human psyche and offering insights into how we can cultivate greater happiness in our lives.

One of the most fascinating findings to emerge from the science of happiness is the concept of the happiness set point—a genetically predetermined baseline for our level of happiness. While this may sound discouraging at first, studies have shown that our happiness set point is not fixed and can be influenced by various external and internal factors, such as our mindset, habits, and social connections.

Moreover, research has identified several key factors that consistently correlate with higher levels of happiness, including:

- Cultivating gratitude and practicing acts of kindness

- Nurturing strong social relationships and fostering a sense of belonging

- Engaging in meaningful activities that align with our values and passions

-        Cultivating mindfulness and savoring the present moment

-        Setting and pursuing achievable goals that provide a sense of purpose and direction

By understanding the science of happiness and incorporating these evidence-based strategies into our lives, we can gradually shift our happiness set point and cultivate a deeper sense of well-being and fulfillment.

Common misconceptions about happiness

Despite our best efforts to understand happiness, there are many common misconceptions that can hinder our ability to experience true joy and fulfillment. One such misconception is the belief that happiness is contingent upon external circumstances, such as wealth, success, or material possessions. While these factors may bring temporary pleasure, they are ultimately fleeting and often fail to provide lasting satisfaction.

Another common misconception is the idea that happiness is a destination to be reached—a final destination where all our problems will magically disappear and we will live happily ever after. In reality, happiness is not a fixed destination but rather a journey—a journey that unfolds moment by moment, requiring us to cultivate awareness, acceptance, and resilience along the way.

Furthermore, many people mistakenly believe that happiness is solely a matter of luck or fate—that some are destined to be happy while others are doomed to a life of misery. While genetics and external circumstances certainly play a role in our overall level of happiness, research has shown that we have far more control over our happiness than we may realize. By adopting a growth mindset and actively practicing happiness-enhancing habits, we can take proactive steps to increase our well-being and live more fulfilling lives.

In conclusion, understanding happiness requires us to redefine our preconceived notions, embrace the science behind them, and cultivate a deeper awareness of our own inner landscape. By doing so, we can unlock the door to true happiness and discover the joy that resides within us all.

CHAPTER TWO

THE HAPPINESS MINDSET

In the pursuit of happiness, our mindset plays a crucial role—a lens through which we view the world and interpret our experiences. Cultivating a happiness mindset involves adopting a set of attitudes and practices that empower us to find joy, meaning, and fulfillment in our everyday lives. In this chapter, we explore the foundational elements of the happiness mindset, focusing on cultivating gratitude and appreciation, practicing mindfulness, adopting a positive outlook, and embracing self-compassion and forgiveness.

Cultivating gratitude and appreciation

Gratitude is a powerful antidote to negativity and dissatisfaction, shifting our focus from what we lack to what we have. Cultivating gratitude involves acknowledging and appreciating the blessings, big and small, that enrich our lives each day.

Take time each day to reflect on the things you're grateful for, whether it's the love of family and friends, the beauty of nature, or the simple pleasures of life. Keep a gratitude journal or make a mental note of three things you're thankful for each day. By cultivating gratitude, you can foster a greater sense of abundance, contentment, and well-being in your life.

Practicing mindfulness and living in the present moment

Mindfulness is the practice of being fully present and engaged in the here and now with an attitude of openness, curiosity, and acceptance. Practicing mindfulness allows us to cultivate greater awareness of our thoughts, feelings, and sensations and to respond to life's challenges with clarity and compassion.

Incorporate mindfulness into your daily routine by taking moments to pause and simply be present. Practice mindful breathing, body scan meditation, or mindful eating to anchor yourself in the present moment and cultivate a sense of inner peace and calm. By practicing mindfulness, you can reduce stress, enhance self-awareness, and savor the richness of each moment.

Adopting a Positive Outlook and Reframing Negative Thoughts

Our thoughts have a powerful influence on our emotions and experiences, shaping our perception of the world and our sense of well-being. Adopting a positive outlook involves cultivating optimism and resilience and reframing negative thoughts in a more constructive and empowering light.

Practice challenging negative thoughts and beliefs by questioning their validity and exploring alternative perspectives. Cultivate a sense of optimism by focusing on solutions rather than problems and by finding opportunities for growth and learning in every situation. By adopting a positive outlook, you can cultivate greater resilience, optimism, and well-being in your life.

Embracing self-compassion and forgiveness

Self-compassion is the practice of treating ourselves with kindness, understanding, and acceptance, especially during times of difficulty or suffering. Embracing self-compassion involves recognizing our common humanity, acknowledging our imperfections, and offering ourselves the same compassion and care we would offer to a loved one.

Practice self-compassion by cultivating self-awareness and self-acceptance and by speaking to yourself with kindness and encouragement. Let go of self-criticism and perfectionism, and embrace the beauty of your imperfections and vulnerabilities. Additionally, practice forgiveness—both towards yourself and others—as a powerful tool for healing and liberation. By embracing self-compassion and forgiveness, you can cultivate greater resilience, self-acceptance, and inner peace in your life.

On a general note, cultivating a happiness mindset is a transformative journey—a journey of self-discovery, growth, and empowerment. By cultivating gratitude and appreciation, practicing mindfulness, adopting a positive outlook, and embracing self-compassion and forgiveness, you can unlock the door to a life filled with joy, meaning, and fulfillment. As you embark on this journey, may you cultivate a mindset of happiness and abundance, and may you find joy and fulfillment in every moment of your life.

CHAPTER THREE

BUILDING POSITIVE RELATIONSHIPS

One of the most important things that affects our happiness in the pursuit of it is the caliber of our connections. Since humans are social creatures by nature, the relationships we have with other people greatly influence how happy, fulfilled, and like we are in the world. This chapter will examine the value of forming wholesome relationships and show us how doing so can significantly improve our quality of life.

Nurturing Meaningful Connections

At the heart of positive relationships lies the deep sense of connection and belonging that we experience when we share our lives with others. Nurturing meaningful connections involves cultivating authentic relationships built on trust, mutual respect, and emotional intimacy. Whether with family members, friends, romantic partners, or colleagues, investing time and effort into building positive relationships can have a transformative impact on our happiness and well-being.

To nurture meaningful connections, it's essential to prioritize communication, empathy, and vulnerability. By actively listening to others, expressing empathy, and sharing our thoughts and feelings openly, we can create a space for deeper connection and understanding to flourish. Additionally, investing in shared experiences and creating lasting memories together can strengthen the bonds of friendship and love, fostering a sense of connection and belonging that sustains us through life's ups and downs.

Communicating Effectively and Resolving Conflicts

Effective communication is the cornerstone of healthy relationships, enabling us to express our needs, desires, and boundaries with clarity and compassion. By practicing active listening, assertive communication, and conflict resolution skills, we can navigate disagreements and misunderstandings with grace and understanding, strengthening our relationships in the process.

When conflicts arise, it's important to approach them with a spirit of openness, empathy, and cooperation. Instead of resorting to blame or defensiveness, we can seek to understand the underlying emotions and needs driving the conflict, finding common ground and mutually beneficial solutions. By approaching conflicts as opportunities for growth and learning rather than threats to our relationships, we can deepen our understanding of ourselves and others, fostering greater harmony and connection.

Setting Boundaries and Prioritizing Self-Care Within Relationships

While nurturing positive relationships is essential for our well-being, it's equally important to set healthy boundaries and prioritize self-care within those relationships. Boundaries help us establish clear expectations and limits around our time, energy, and resources, ensuring that our needs are met and our values respected.

Setting boundaries may involve saying no to requests that drain our energy or compromise our values, communicating our needs and preferences assertively, and advocating for our well-being without guilt or apology. By honoring our boundaries and prioritizing self-care within our relationships, we can cultivate a greater sense of balance, autonomy, and fulfillment, enabling us to show up as our best selves in our interactions with others.

In a nutshell, building positive relationships is a cornerstone of happiness and well-being, enriching our lives with love, connection, and support. By nurturing meaningful connections, communicating effectively, and prioritizing self-care within our relationships, we can create a life filled with joy, fulfillment, and meaningful connection. As we cultivate positive relationships with others, may we also cultivate a deeper sense of connection with ourselves, honoring our needs, values, and aspirations with compassion and authenticity.

CHAPTER FOUR

FINDING PURPOSE AND MEANING

In the vast landscape of human existence, finding purpose and meaning serves as the compass that guides us through life's journey, illuminating our path and infusing each step with significance and fulfillment. In this chapter, we delve deep into the pursuit of purpose and meaning, exploring the essential steps of identifying personal values and passions, setting meaningful goals, and embracing the transformative power of giving back to others.

Identifying Personal Values and Passions

At the heart of finding purpose and meaning lies a profound understanding of our personal values and passions—the driving forces that shape our beliefs, aspirations, and sense of fulfillment. Identifying our values and passions requires introspection, reflection, and a willingness to explore the depths of our being.

Start by asking yourself probing questions such as "What principles do I hold dear?" "What activities or experiences bring me the most joy and fulfillment?" and "What impact do I want to have on the world?" Through this introspective journey, you'll begin to uncover the core values and passions that resonate deeply with your authentic self.

By aligning your actions and choices with your values and passions, you can infuse your life with a profound sense of purpose and direction, guiding you towards a path of fulfillment and significance.

Setting meaningful goals and pursuing them with intention

With a clear understanding of your values and passions, the next step is to set meaningful goals that reflect your aspirations and contribute to your sense of purpose and fulfillment. Meaningful goals are those that inspire growth, challenge you to reach beyond your comfort zone, and align with your values and passions.

When setting goals, it's essential to follow the SMART criteria—specific, measurable, achievable, relevant, and time-bound. Break down your overarching aspirations into actionable steps and commit to pursuing them with intention and determination.

By approaching your goals with clarity, focus, and perseverance, you can transform your dreams into reality, creating a life that is rich with purpose, meaning, and fulfillment.

Giving back to others and contributing to something greater than oneself

An integral part of finding purpose and meaning lies in giving back to others and contributing to something greater than oneself. Acts of kindness, compassion, and service not only benefit those in need but also enrich your life with a profound sense of connection, fulfillment, and purpose.

Look for opportunities to give back to your community, whether through volunteering, supporting charitable organizations, or simply lending a helping hand to those in need. By sharing your time, talents, and resources with others, you can make a positive impact on the world and leave a lasting legacy that extends far beyond your own lifetime.

Embrace the transformative power of giving back, and discover the joy and fulfillment that come from contributing to something greater than yourself. As you journey through life, may you find purpose and meaning in every moment, and may your actions reflect the depth of your values, passions, and commitment to making the world a better place.

In general, the search for meaning and purpose is an intensely personal and transforming journey that challenges you to reach new heights in your life, make audacious plans, and believe in the transformational power of contribution and service. It is possible to open the door to a happy, fulfilling life by discovering your values and passions, making meaningful goals, and volunteering. May you seize the chance to design a life that is genuinely meaningful—one that captures the spirit of who you are and the influence you hope to make on the world—as you set out on this journey.

CHAPTER FIVE

CULTIVATING JOY IN DAILY LIFE

In the hustle and bustle of modern life, finding moments of joy and contentment can often feel like a fleeting pursuit. Yet, amidst the chaos, there exists a profound opportunity to cultivate joy in our daily lives—a practice that can transform even the most mundane moments into sources of inspiration and delight. In this section, we explore the art of cultivating joy in daily life through mindfulness practices, embracing simple pleasures, pursuing fulfilling activities, and finding balance amidst life's challenges.

Incorporating mindfulness practices into daily routines

Mindfulness is the practice of being fully present and engaged in the present moment, with an attitude of openness, curiosity, and acceptance. By incorporating mindfulness practices into our daily routines, we can cultivate a deeper sense of awareness, peace, and joy in our lives.

Start by carving out moments of stillness and silence in your day—whether through meditation, deep breathing exercises, or simply taking a few moments to pause and observe your surroundings. Tune into your senses, noticing the sights, sounds, smells, and sensations around you with curiosity and appreciation.

As you go about your daily activities, strive to bring mindfulness to each moment, whether you're eating a meal, washing the dishes, or walking in nature. By cultivating a sense of presence and intentionality in your actions, you can transform even the most ordinary tasks into opportunities for joy and connection with the world around you.

Finding Joy in Simple Pleasures and Moments of Beauty

In our fast-paced society, it's easy to overlook the simple pleasures and moments of beauty that surround us each day. Yet, these small moments—whether it's a warm cup of tea, a breathtaking sunset, or a heartfelt conversation with a loved one—have the power to nourish our souls and infuse our lives with joy and gratitude.

Take time each day to savor the simple pleasures and moments of beauty that cross your path. Pause to appreciate the beauty of nature, the warmth of the sun on your skin, or the laughter of children playing in the park. Cultivate an attitude of gratitude for the abundance of beauty and wonder that surrounds you, and allow yourself to be fully present in each moment.

By finding joy in the simple pleasures of life, you can cultivate a sense of appreciation and wonder that enriches your daily experience and brings a smile to your face.

Pursuing Hobbies and Activities That Bring Fulfillment

One of the most effective ways to cultivate joy in daily life is by pursuing hobbies and activities that bring you a sense of fulfillment and joy. Whether it's painting, gardening, playing music, or exploring the great outdoors, engaging in activities that nourish your passions and interests can provide a much-needed source of joy and rejuvenation.

Take time each day to engage in activities that bring you joy and fulfillment, even if it's just for a few minutes. Whether it's starting a new creative project, going for a walk in nature, or spending time with loved ones, prioritize activities that nourish your soul and bring you a sense of joy and fulfillment.

By making time for activities that bring you joy, you can cultivate a greater sense of purpose and meaning in your life and infuse each day with a sense of excitement and possibility.

Managing stress and finding balance in life

In our fast-paced world, stress and overwhelm can often overshadow our ability to experience joy and contentment. Yet, by managing stress and finding balance in our lives, we can create space for joy to flourish and cultivate a greater sense of well-being.

Practice self-care rituals such as exercise, meditation, or spending time in nature to help alleviate stress and promote relaxation. Set boundaries around your time and energy, prioritizing activities that bring you joy and fulfillment while also honoring your need for rest and rejuvenation.

By finding balance in your life and prioritizing activities that nourish your body, mind, and spirit, you can create a foundation for joy to thrive and experience greater levels of happiness and fulfillment.

Conclusively, cultivating joy in daily life is a practice—an ongoing journey of presence, appreciation, and intentionality. By incorporating mindfulness practices into your daily routines, embracing simple pleasures, pursuing fulfilling activities, and finding balance amidst life's challenges, you can unlock the door to a life filled with joy, contentment, and meaning. As you embark on this journey, may you find joy in the ordinary moments of life, and may each day be a celebration of the beauty and wonder that surrounds you.

CHAPTER SIX

OVERCOMING OBSTACLES TO HAPPINESS

In our journey towards happiness, we inevitably encounter obstacles—challenges, setbacks, and inner demons—that threaten to derail our pursuit of joy and fulfillment. Yet, it is in the face of these obstacles that we have the opportunity to cultivate resilience, strength, and inner peace. Now, let us look at some of the common barriers to happiness, strategies for dealing with setbacks and adversity, and the importance of seeking professional help when needed to destigmatize mental health support.

Addressing common barriers to happiness

1. Perfectionism: The relentless pursuit of perfection can be a significant barrier to happiness, as it often leads to unrealistic expectations, self-criticism, and a constant sense of dissatisfaction. Recognize that perfection can be achieved with continuous practice, and embrace the beauty of imperfection while growing. Practice self-compassion and celebrate your efforts and progress, no matter how small.

2. Comparison: Constantly comparing ourselves to others can breed feelings of inadequacy, envy, and self-doubt, undermining our sense of happiness and well-being. Shift your focus inward and cultivate self-awareness and self-acceptance. Celebrate your unique strengths, talents, and accomplishments, and avoid the temptation to measure your worth against others.

3. Fear: Fear of failure, rejection, or uncertainty can hold us back from pursuing our dreams and living authentically, preventing us from experiencing true happiness and fulfillment. Challenge your fears by taking small, courageous steps outside your comfort zone. Cultivate a growth mindset and view failure as an opportunity for growth and learning rather than a reflection of your worth.

Strategies for Dealing with Setbacks and Adversity

1. Practice resilience: Reframe setbacks as chances for personal development and education to cultivate resilience. Instead of focusing on difficulties, adopt an optimistic outlook and concentrate on finding solutions. Make use of your assets, network of allies, and prior triumphs over hardship to get through trying times with poise and fortitude.

2. Cultivate self-care: Prioritize self-care practices such as exercise, meditation, and spending time in nature to nurture your physical, mental, and emotional well-being. Make time for activities that bring you joy and relaxation, and honor your need for rest and rejuvenation during difficult times.

3. Foster social support: Lean on your support network of friends, family, and loved ones during times of adversity. Reach out for help when needed, and be open to receiving support and encouragement from others. Cultivate deep, meaningful connections that provide comfort, understanding, and companionship during challenging times.

Seeking Professional Help When Needed and Destigmatizing Mental Health Support

1. Break the stigma: Challenge societal taboos and stereotypes surrounding mental health by openly discussing your struggles and seeking support when needed. Educate yourself and others about the importance of mental health and the availability of resources and support services.
2. Reach out for help: Don't hesitate to seek professional help from therapists, counselors, or mental health professionals if you're struggling to cope with obstacles to happiness. Therapy can provide a safe space to explore your thoughts and feelings, develop coping strategies, and work towards greater well-being and fulfillment.
3. Prioritize self-care: Make self-care a priority in your life and seek out activities and practices that nourish your body, mind, and spirit. Whether it's exercise, meditation, creative expression, or spending time with loved ones, prioritize activities that bring you joy, relaxation, and inner peace.

Overcoming obstacles to happiness is a journey—a journey of self-discovery, growth, and resilience. By addressing common barriers such as perfectionism, comparison, and fear, practicing strategies for dealing with setbacks and adversity, and seeking professional help when needed, you can unlock the door to a life filled with joy, fulfillment, and inner peace. As you navigate the challenges of life, may you cultivate resilience, strength, and compassion, and may you find happiness in the face of adversity.

CHAPTER SEVEN

SUSTAINING LONG-TERM HAPPINESS

Happiness is not merely a destination but a journey—a journey marked by growth, resilience, and a commitment to living authentically and joyfully. In this final chapter, we delve into the art of sustaining long-term happiness, exploring the importance of creating habits and rituals that support happiness, continuously learning and growing emotionally, and fostering resilience in the face of life's challenges.

Creating Habits and Rituals that Support Happiness

1. Daily Gratitude Practice: Include a daily gratitude exercise in your routine to help you develop an attitude of gratitude. Every day, set aside some time to think about the things you have to be grateful for, such as your loved ones, the wonders of the natural world, or the small things in life. Regular thankfulness practice can help you develop a more abundant mindset as well as a greater sense of contentment and wellbeing.

2. Mindfulness Meditation: Integrate mindfulness meditation into your daily life to cultivate present-moment awareness and inner peace. Set

aside time each day to practice mindfulness meditation, focusing on your breath, body sensations, or surroundings. By bringing your attention back to the present moment, you can reduce stress, increase resilience, and enhance your overall sense of happiness and fulfillment.

3. Acts of Kindness: Make a habit of performing random acts of kindness and generosity towards others. Whether it's offering a helping hand to a stranger, writing a heartfelt note to a friend, or volunteering your time for a worthy cause, acts of kindness can not only brighten someone else's day but also boost your own happiness and sense of purpose.

Continuous learning and emotional growth

1. Cultivate Curiosity: Embrace a lifelong commitment to learning and personal growth by cultivating curiosity and openness to new experiences. Explore new interests, hobbies, and skills that challenge and inspire you, and approach life with a sense of wonder and curiosity. By expanding your knowledge and perspective, you can enrich your life with meaning, purpose, and joy.

2. Emotional Intelligence: Develop your emotional intelligence by honing your ability to recognize, understand, and manage your emotions effectively. Practice self-awareness and self-reflection to gain insight into your thoughts, feelings, and behaviors, and cultivate empathy and compassion towards yourself and others. By developing emotional intelligence, you can navigate relationships with greater ease,

resilience, and authenticity, enhancing your overall sense of happiness and well-being.

Fostering resilience and adapting to life's challenges

1. Embrace Change: Embrace change as a natural part of life and an opportunity for growth and transformation. Instead of resisting change, cultivate flexibility and adaptability, and approach life's challenges with an attitude of curiosity and resilience. By embracing change with an open heart and mind, you can navigate transitions with greater ease and grace and emerge stronger and more resilient in the process.
2. Cultivate support networks: Surround yourself with supportive friends, family, and mentors who can offer guidance, encouragement, and perspective during challenging times. Cultivate deep, meaningful connections that provide comfort, understanding, and companionship, and lean on your support network for strength and resilience when faced with adversity.
3. Practice self-compassion: Be gentle and compassionate with yourself during times of difficulty and struggle. Practice self-care rituals that nourish your body, mind, and spirit, and offer yourself kindness and understanding in moments of pain and self-doubt. By cultivating self-compassion, you can build resilience and inner strength and navigate life's challenges with greater ease and grace.

In essence, maintaining long-term happiness requires a journey—a continuous process of development, resiliency, and self-awareness. You can open the door to a life full of joy, purpose, and fulfillment by developing routines and habits that promote happiness, consistently learning and developing emotionally, and building resilience in the face of adversity. May you develop resilience, welcome change, and fill your soul with love, thankfulness, and compassion as you set out on your path.

CHAPTER EIGHT

EMBRACING HAPPINESS

As we reach the conclusion of our journey together, I invite you to take a moment to reflect on the path we've traveled and the insights we've uncovered. Throughout this book, we've explored various strategies for unlocking happiness—strategies that have the power to transform your life and infuse each day with joy, meaning, and fulfillment. Now, as we bid farewell, let us recap the key strategies for embracing happiness, encourage you to take action, and express hope for a brighter, happier future.

Summarizing Key Strategies for Unlocking Happiness

1. Cultivate Mindfulness: Practice being fully present in the moment, embracing each experience with curiosity, openness, and acceptance.
2. Nurture Positive Relationships: Prioritize meaningful connections with others, fostering trust, empathy, and mutual respect in your interactions.
3. Find Purpose and Meaning: Identify your values and passions, set meaningful goals, and contribute to something greater than yourself.

4. Cultivate Joy in Daily Life: Incorporate mindfulness practices, savor simple pleasures, pursue fulfilling activities, and manage stress to nurture happiness in your daily life.
5. Overcome Obstacles: Address common barriers such as perfectionism, comparison, and fear, and develop resilience to navigate setbacks and challenges with grace.
6. Sustain Long-Term Happiness: Create habits and rituals that support happiness, continuously learn and grow emotionally, and foster resilience in the face of life's challenges.

Call to Action

Now that you've gained valuable insights and strategies for unlocking happiness, I encourage you to take action and implement what you've learned into your daily life. Start by identifying one key strategy that resonates with you and committing to incorporating it into your routine. Whether it's practicing gratitude, nurturing relationships, or pursuing your passions, take small, actionable steps towards greater happiness and fulfillment each day.

Remember that change takes time and effort, so be patient and compassionate with yourself as you embark on this journey. Celebrate your progress and learn from setbacks, knowing that every step forward brings you closer to a happier and more fulfilling life.

Expressing Hope for a Happier and More Fulfilling Life for the Reader

As you close the final chapter of this book, I want to express my sincerest hope for a happier and more fulfilling life for you, dear reader. May you embrace the strategies for unlocking happiness with an open heart and mind, knowing that you deserve joy, fulfillment, and inner peace.

May you find the courage to take bold steps towards a brighter future, knowing that happiness is not a destination but a journey—a journey that begins with a single step and unfolds with each moment of presence, connection, and gratitude.

May your life be filled with love, laughter, and moments of profound joy, and may you always remember that happiness is not something to be pursued but a state of being to be embraced and cultivated each day.

As you embark on this new chapter of your journey, may you walk with confidence, purpose, and a deep sense of inner peace, knowing that the key to unlocking happiness lies within you.

Farewell, dear reader, and may your life be filled with abundant happiness and fulfillment.